11-17-67

# LIVING THE CHRISTIAN SEASONS

# LIVING THE CHRISTIAN SEASONS

CHARLES K. RIEPE

HERDER AND HERDER

1964
HERDER AND HERDER NEW YORK
232 Madison Avenue, New York 16, N.Y.


Nihil obstat:    Carroll E. Satterfield
                 Censor Librorum

Imprimatur:  ✝Lawrence J. Shehan
                 Archbishop of Baltimore

             June 12, 1964

Library of Congress Catalog Card Number: 64–19734
© 1964 by Herder and Herder, Incorporated
Printed in the United States of America

C690071

# Contents

# FOREWORD

In the Constitution on the Sacred Liturgy, the expression "paschal mystery" appears more than once as a key word. This little book on the Church Year might well be considered a commentary on this expression.

The work of a busy diocesan priest, it reveals a notable understanding of the origin and meaning of the individual feasts of the Church Year. It becomes clear in these pages that the feasts of the Church are not merely subjective memories of past events but are full of meaning and vitality for the present. Both the knowledge and attainment of these realities are obviously of the greatest importance for the Church feasts to achieve their full fruit.

It is also clear that the Church Year is not composed simply of a series of unrelated happenings in the earthly life of Christ. Rather it consists of a unified presentation of the paschal mystery for the participation and formation of the faithful.

May this little book assist in the learning of these important lessons.

Josef A. Jungmann, S.J.
Innsbruck, Austria
May 1964

# INTRODUCTION

This little book has but one purpose and one message: to show the Catholic lay person that the Church year presents the mystery of the redemption for our understanding and participation; one message, it would seem, is enough for one book.

Most of what is presented here first appeared in the *Baltimore Catholic Review* in the form of a weekly column. It does not represent an original contribution to Liturgical Science but merely attempts to utilize the findings of others in the process of adult Christian formation.

The author hopes that converts and others not of our communion will find it useful.

CHARLES K. RIEPE

*Baltimore 1964*

## 1

# A Simple Theology of the Church Year

One of the basic principles employed in the liturgy of the Church is the principle of liturgical explanation. In other words the Church by outward rites and gestures explains the inward happenings of the liturgy. Usually however the essential sacramental event takes place so quickly—and of course invisibly—that the congregation is often unaware of when it has ended. Since this might easily cause confusion, and even disappointment, the Church acts out the sacramental event so that all those present can have some idea of what has occurred.

During the administration of the sacrament of baptism, for example, the actual baptism consists in the pouring of the water and the recitation of the words "I baptize you . . ." The baptism takes place within a matter of seconds. But the Church does not end the baptismal rite immediately after the moment of baptism. She goes on to explain by means of liturgical rites what has happened in those few seconds: the person is anointed with oil to signify the share in Christ's priesthood which we all receive in baptism; the white robe symbolic of purity and innocence is given the newly baptized; and finally he is presented the lighted candle symbolizing that Christ the light of the world and the light of faith is enkindled in our souls and bodies in baptism.

All these things—the conferring of a share in Christ's priesthood, the putting on of purity and innocence, the enkindling of faith, etc.—all these things occurred in those few seconds when the water was poured and the words recited. But the Church explains what happened in those seconds by acting it out in the liturgy.

The same is true of the sacrament of holy orders. The actual ordination to the priesthood takes place in a matter of seconds, yet the ceremony lasts for some two hours. Everything that happens after the actual ordination, such as the conferring of the chalice and paten, the pronouncement of the words "Whose sins you shall forgive . . ." is simply a liturgical explanation of what happened in the actual moment of ordination.

In short then, because the human mind is so limited and can only grasp so much at a time, the liturgical explanation makes the mysteries of our faith more intelligible by using words, gestures and rites to show what happens in the administration of a sacrament. This same principle of liturgical explanation can also be applied to the Church year.

Basically the Church year is one grand liturgical explanation of the central truth of the Catholic faith: the death and resurrection of Jesus Christ by which the redemption was accomplished. The Church explains this great truth by showing us what led up to and what came after it. In other words the Church year is the great liturgical explanation of the mystery of Easter: the redemption. Easter is at the heart of the Church year, and it is around Easter that the Church revolves. This truth is clearly demonstrated by the history of the Church year.

The oldest liturgical book of the western Church, a book of scripture readings called a lectionary, begins and ends with Easter. Patristic references strengthen this position. For instance Pseudo Ambrosius remarks that "the pasch is truly the beginning of the year." Augustine takes up the same theme: "Because of the beginning of the new life . . . , because of the new life itself, the first among the months of the year is given over to this celebration. For it is called the month of the things made new." Nor can one disregard the ancient notion that God created the world in the springtime; and since it was also in the spring that he redeemed it, it seemed eminently fitting that this season should be the beginning of the yearly cycle.

This theme is also found in a sermon by Leo the Great: "Now at this feast sacred among all feasts, the month of things made new is radiant with light, so that the month in which the world had its beginning might also be the one in which the Christian creation began." For Cyril of Alexandria Easter is "the beginning of a new era (aeon)."

For more than three hundred years no other feast was celebrated in the Catholic Church apart from Easter. The first record of Christmas is in the year 335–6. The death and resurrection of Christ was celebrated solemnly once a year at Easter, and celebrated in less solemn fashion once every week on Sunday.

### Sunday: Church Year in Miniature

The Sunday celebration of Easter is a most ancient and significant feature of the Church year. Each Sunday in the year was a "little Easter" just as every Friday was a "little Good Friday"—a fact impressed on us since earliest times by the sacrifice of abstaining from meat. By the very fact that every Sunday is a little Easter it is also a sort of Church year in miniature.

The best evidence for the Church's outlook on the Sunday observance is found in the names she employs for the day itself. One of the oldest names for Sunday, a name used in the New Testament and still used today, is the lord's day. For Paul the term lord was a special designation for Christ. The Greek word kyrios (lord) contains great power and force: it refers to Jesus as the risen and victorious one, as the lord of life who has triumphed over the grave. Thus the lord's day actually means Christ's day, the day dedicated to him as victor and risen one. To many of us the term lord's day seems Protestant; yet to this day in the western Church the official name for sunday is Dies Dominica, the lord's day.

One of the most striking expressions for Sunday is found among the Greeks: resurrection day, a term also used among the Russians. Another patristic expression which brings out the same idea is the eighth day. The idea was that God completed his work of creation in six days and rested on the seventh, the Jewish sabbath. But God went on to continue his work of salvation on the following day, our Sunday, and to an earlier age the day on which Jesus rose was a continuation of God's work. Thus it was the eighth day. For this reason many an early baptistry was built in an octagonal shape to symbolize Jesus' resurrection on the eighth day.

To Christian antiquity Sunday was the end of the week, the eighth day. Because the Jewish way of reckoning was so familiar the Church retained in her official terminology the expression second day for Monday, third day for Tuesday, and so on. But among some peoples, such as the Lithuanians, the word for Monday—pirmadienis—literally means first day, and the Hungarian word for Monday means head of the week.

The word Sunday also has a profound Christian-Easter meaning. Sunday of course is the day of the sun: the sun cult was a very practiced one in ancient Rome. Rather than try to forbid the Christians to have anything to do with the idea of the sun the Church christianized it. Jesus, they said, is the true sun who will never set. And just as the sun in the sky sinks each evening into the west and, according to the ancients, descends into the underworld before rising in the morning with new brilliance to bring light to the earth, so too did Jesus. For he too after he had died on the cross "descended into hell" before rising with new life and power on Sunday morning. Thus the early Christians had no difficulty in adjusting to the use of the word Sunday in their own observance.

Sunday therefore is really resurrection day, a little Easter. Its main theme is the resurrection of the lord and, truly, the whole Easter mystery. And since it is around this theme that the whole Church year revolves each Sunday can thus be properly called a Church year in miniature.


### Characteristics of the Church Year

While Easter and its weekly celebration were for some time the only Christian feast, it was only natural that as time went on other feasts would be added to the Church year. But what we have lost sight of today is the fact that these additions of the past seventeen hundred years have a definite place in the scheme of things and are not just feasts unto themselves with no relationship to anything else. The theme and central mystery of the Church year remains the redemption.

For instance there is no such thing as a feast of a divine person unto himself (e.g. the feast of God the father); rather the three divine persons are venerated in the role that is their's in the work of redemption. Even the feasts of the saints relate in some way to redemption. The various seasons which take events in the life of Jesus as their themes are celebrated because they pertain in some way to the redeemer's mission of salvation.

It is impossible for the human mind to have the entire plan of Jesus' work of redemption in focus at any one moment, to see the work of redemption in its entirety all at once. The Church year spreads the entire work of Jesus over a year's time so that we may contemplate the whole of God's plan for our salvation which was realized in his son. In the course of the year the Church gives us the opportunity to hear and digest the mystery of the redemption in its totality so that we may realize the extent of God's love for us.

At Christmas we see the person of the savior who brings us the message of salvation from God the father. Beginning with Septuagesima we trace the actual work of redemption on through to the coming of the Holy Spirit at Pentecost, which is also part of the Easter experience. After Pentecost we apply to our own lives the fruit of what Jesus came to give and do for us. Finally, during advent, we turn our attention to his final coming and prepare for the judgment that awaits us. The various feasts of Mary and Joseph remind us throughout the year of Jesus' first coming and of the person who is our savior. The feasts of the other saints, the confessors, martyrs, virgins, etc. illustrate clearly the way of life he came to show us, and the fruit of the redemption that he worked.

From what we have said it would appear a mistake to see in the Church year some fanciful portrayal of the earthly life of Christ pure and simple. The Church year is not an attempt simply to relive the earthly life of Jesus by way of chronological sequence. Rather the Church year is the placing before us of the mystery of redemption, of Easter, in such a way that we may contemplate it in its totality and actively participate in it. In a word it is the liturgical explanation of Easter whose vast implications and parts would overwhelm us if we had to take them in all at once. The Church year provides us with one triumphal celebration of redemption which is the very core of our life and worship. By participating in the Church year in this spirit we will find, rather than a series of unrelated if beautiful events, a Christian truth easily tangible and readily usable in our spiritual lives. And we will be learning about God and his son as they themselves have taught us.

## Arranging the Church Year

Basically the question involved here is when the Church year begins and ends. The question however is primarily academic since we are not dealing in the Church year with the life of Jesus in the strict chronological order as an end in itself. Rather, as we noted above, the purpose of the Church year is to place before us the mystery of our redemption. The redemption is not something with a beginning and an end but, like a circle, something which can be contemplated from any point or aspect.

For the sake of logic however we propose to begin our examination of the Church year with Christmas. This order dates from the fourth and fifth centuries, although it is not the primitive order; in the beginning the Church year began and ended with Easter. And we should keep in mind that the terms Church year and starting and ending, familiar to us today, were in this context meaningless in early times. In the primitive Christian community there was no Church year as such apart from the calendar year. Not until 1589 does the term Church year first appear. Some of the early Christian books simply began with January. And the question of beginning and ending was pertinent only insofar as those who compiled the early books had to have some place to begin! The majority of western liturgical books which have come down to us show a preference for beginning at

Christmas, or more exactly its vigil. The sacramentaries usually begin in this manner but the oldest of them, the Leonianum, must have begun in January—the first three months are missing in the oldest extant manuscript, but it is arranged according to months and ends in December. Most antiphonals begin either with what is our present advent or with what is now the last Sunday after Pentecost. The lectionaries prefer Christmas over advent, and in these books the lists of saints' feasts begin with Dec 26, which is logical if Christmas is taken as the starting point. And since advent is a later development, and since its main theme is the *end*, we will close our discussion with it. Such an arrangement, we hope, will serve to deepen our understanding of the mystery of the redemption as the Church teaches it throughout the year.

## 2

# THE COMING OF THE REDEEMER

## Christmas

The celebration of the birth of Jesus was not a part of the primitive Roman liturgy. Actually the feast of the Epiphany is older. The early Church only celebrated Easter and its weekly commemoration every Sunday. Probably the next item to be added to the Church year was the santification of the seasons, the ember days.

The first reference to the observance of Christmas is found in a document called the *Despositio Martyrum,* a list of martyrs' feasts drawn up for the use of the Roman Church. In a sense it was an early Church calendar. This document dates from 335–6 and begins with Christmas. The precise date given is Dec 25.

Why was it not until the middle of the fourth century that the Church began to celebrate Christmas? And why was the twenty-fifth day of December chosen?

This aspect of the Christmas feast is perhaps the most prominent example of missionary adaptation in the entire Roman liturgy. For in Rome Dec 25 was the pagan celebration of the birth of the sol invictus, the sun, worshiped as a god, and whose cult was quite popular at the time. The nativity was a christianization of this pagan feast. The Church found the sun cult difficult to ignore and so decided that for the Christian Dec 25 should be the birth of Jesus, the true light of the world. The early Christians had little difficulty in adopting the sun as a symbol of Christ, for as we have already noted the ancients believed that the sun descends into the underworld before rising again in the east with new light and brilliance. So too did Christ, the "true sun who will never set," slowly fade and sink to his death on the cross. He too descended into the underworld and arose in new life and splendor on Easter morning.

Thus the rising sun became the symbol of Jesus Christ, and Dec 25 became his birthday. And while it is correct to assume that the celebration of Jesus' birth was bound to be observed, still it took a pagan feast to be the occasion for its institution.

The celebration of Christmas did not have the proportions in those days that it has today. We are accustomed to speak of Christmas eve as the holy night, whereas this term to an earlier Christian could only have meant one thing: the Easter vigil. However it was only natural that during the fourth and fifth centuries, with the Church's anti-Arian emphasis on the person of Jesus, with his divinity being more and more stressed, the events of his earthly life took on greater significance. And after all it was God himself who was born, who was taken into Egypt, who was baptized by John the Baptist.

Thus a whole new cycle of feasts developed which pertained in some way to the Christmas feast: the feast of

John the Baptist, the visitation, the purification, the annunciation, the feast of Joseph. Thus the feast of Christmas itself took on new importance. And under the impetus of Francis of Assisi the Christmas crib added much warmth to the feast.

The real meaning of the feast of Christmas is found in the word incarnation, for in the incarnation God intervened most radically in the affairs of the human race by sending his own divine son to become a true man in order to effect our salvation. In the incarnation God inaugurated in a striking manner the principle according to which he would lead men back to himself. That principle is simply that God the uncreated and invisible would employ the created and visible to effect the salvation of mankind. This is the principle of the incarnation and it is embodied in Jesus Christ. In Jesus the man God has not only appeared to man but has actually redeemed him. It is the humanity of Jesus which ascended the cross, rose from the dead and ascended into heaven. Jesus in his humanity was (and is) something created, taken from the virgin Mary, clearly visible and human in all things except sin. This created, visible humanity was used by God in carrying out his plan for our redemption.

But the application of the principle does not stop with the humanity of Jesus. The Church herself follows this same pattern for she too is something created, she too is something visible, something external. Yet just as the humanity of Jesus was the outward sign for the invisible divinity, so too is the Church an outward sign for the invisible presence of Jesus in the world. She too is something visible designed by God to lead men back to himself, the invisible.

The application of the principle of the incarnation continues clearly in the sacraments of the Church. Here again the created, the earthly, the visible (bread, wine, water, oil, etc) are employed as outward signs for invisible realities leading men to God, and indeed constituting man's closest contact with God in this world. Thomas Aquinas has pointed out that it is symbolic of man's humility as a creature that he is dependent on other earthly things in his approach to God.

In discussing the real meaning of Christmas we should not overlook the question of faith. Those who came to the manger of Bethlehem and professed their faith in the new born king did so primarily out of faith. It was not until centuries later that Christian art gave us the image of the birth of Jesus that we now have. With the exception of the virgin birth itself the nativity was a strictly human operation. Those who came to pay homage saw only an infant, no more and no less. It was faith in God and his word which led them to confess their belief that this baby was the redeemer of the world.

Today God continues by means of the incarnation to lead us to salvation. It requires faith to know that beneath the veils of bread and wine Jesus is really and truly present. It requires faith to realize that the priest is working and acting in the place of Jesus and that something is happening which the eye cannot see.

On Christmas day a priest is permitted to celebrate three masses. This custom is first referred to by Gregory the

Great in one of his sermons wherein he mentions that as pope he conducts three stational services on Christmas day. In time all priests began offering three masses on this day whether they conducted public services or not.

Of the three masses the oldest is the third mass, which was originally celebrated on Christmas morning. The gospel used is still the prologue of John with its famous phrase "the word was made flesh and dwelt among us" which characterizes the Roman idea of a feast.

The next mass to be added was what is now the first mass or the midnight mass. This scheduling for midnight was done in imitation of the midnight mass celebrated at Bethlehem at the place of the savior's birth. And it was in imitation of this grotto in Bethlehem that the Church of St Mary Major in Rome was constructed.

The third mass to be added is what is now the second mass; its origins go back to the days of the byzantine influence in Rome in the second half of the sixth century. The orientals had a great devotion to Anastasia, and in deference to them mass was also celebrated in the Church of St Anastasia. Gradually, as the orientals became more accustomed to Christmas, this third mass became a Christmas mass with a commemoration of Anastasia.

## The Octave of Christmas

The octave of Christmas is Jan 1, until recently known as the feast of the circumcision. By the reform of 1960 this name was dropped. It was a non-Roman designation which dated from around the sixth century but which did not make its appearance in the Roman liturgy until the ninth century. The idea of a feast of the circumcision of Jesus presents some delicate questions and also seems to indicate that the whole Christmas theme is a step by step reliving of the earthly events surrounding his birth.

Prior to the ninth century Jan 1 was simply known as the octave of the lord—an octave which had managed to survive for three hundred years without concluding with a feast of the circumcision. Obviously the framers of the 1960 reform felt that the term octave of the nativity was sufficient.

January 1 does remain a holy day of obligation, at least for the present time. This fact lends even more dignity and emphasis to the feast of the incarnation. The Roman liturgy has never taken any formal cognizance of Jan 1 as the beginning of the calendar year. There is no relationship in the liturgy between new year's day and the octave of the nativity. It seems a pity that these two celebrations could not somehow be combined or that the former could not at least gain some recognition. Interestingly enough however the oldest of the sacramentaries, the Leonine, appears to begin with Jan 1 since the rest of the book is ordered according to the months of the calendar year.

## Epiphany

The history and meaning of the feast of the Epiphany is not as simple and clear cut as was the case with Christmas. A number of factors enter into our celebration of the feast, and we will have to try to piece them together in an intelligible manner.

Epiphany is a Greek word which primarily means appearance, or in this case the appearance of God among men. In German the feast is often called simply Erscheinung or appearance. The feast was well known in the Orient in the middle of the third century and was to that day more or less what Christmas is to us. But as was often the case with eastern feasts the Epiphany stressed more the divinity of Jesus, the coming down of God to dwell among men, whereas the western feast of Christmas stresses his humanity, his birth from the virgin Mary.

The date for the feast of the Epiphany, Jan 6, is also an illustration of the christianization of a pagan celebration. The pagan celebration of the winter equinox was celebrated on a day which later came to be Jan 6 in the Julian calendar. Commenting on this pagan celebration Josef Jungmann notes: "On this day, or rather during the night, processions were held in the temples amidst the cries, 'the virgin has brought forth; the light is increasing'. Or according to another version 'The Virgin has brought forth another aeon'."[1] This feast must also have been associated with the feast of the sun god Osiris, who was highly venerated in Egypt. The appearance of the sun, which now begins to grow stronger as the days become longer, and the appearance of Jesus, whom the sun symbolized, were a natural union. The preface for the Epiphany still speaks of the only begotten son "appearing" in our mortal nature.

Still another pagan belief connected with this day was

[1] J. A. Jungmann, *The Early Liturgy*, Notre Dame 1959, 149.

that certain miraculous springs yielded wine instead of water. Thus the day was connected by the Church with the miracle of Cana. And the association with water naturally led to a further association with baptism: the waters of baptism are miraculous because they bring life. They enlighten man, and thus they bring light to the world. Indeed the early Christians called baptism enlightenment.

The picture is further complicated by the fact that the baptism of Jesus was also associated with this feast. In allowing himself to be baptized in the waters of the Jordan Jesus also cleanses his spouse, the Church. Thus the marriage of Christ and his Church is also considered. In the breviary the antiphon for the benedictus on the feast of the Epiphany reads: "Today the Church is joined with her heavenly Spouse, for in the Jordan Christ cleansed her of sin; the Magi hastened with gifts to the royal wedding, and from the water made wine the festivities are celebrated." Thus the Roman liturgy sums up in one antiphon all the elements associated with the feast. Since the 1960 reform Jan 13 has been designated the special commemoration of the baptism of Jesus.

But what of the wise men? We are accustomed to think of Jan 6 as the feast of the wise men who came bearing gifts, who followed "his star in the east." This story however, contained in the gospel of the feast, is merely intended to show how the son of God came to save all men, regardless of race, nationality, etc.

The use of Ps 71, which speaks of the kings coming with gifts, has also given the wise men due prominence. But it was not really until 1164 that their cult began to take on greater proportions, and this was due mainly to the fact that Frederick Barbarossa transferred the "relics" of the wise men from Milan to Cologne, where they repose to this day. This transfer was a great impetus to the devotion and legend which has come to be attached to these three mysterious figures of the gospel.

## The Feasts of Mary

In addition to being a round the year echo of the Christmas theme the feasts of Mary also serve as a reminder of the role she played in the redemptive work of her son. The key to an understanding of the Church's veneration of Mary is precisely Mary in the service of the redemption.

Mary represents the most perfect member of the Church. She is not something apart from the Church or even above it. She is in it, she helped to make it what it is. Like us she too was redeemed, albeit in a different manner. But unlike us her association with Christ was physical to a most intimate degree. Much of what we the Church do today sacramentally, much of what we believe by faith, Mary experienced physically in such a way that we can consider her a sort of forerunner of those of us who are the Church of Jesus Christ.

In her immaculate conception for instance Mary prefigured the immaculate conception of the Church, for the Church is born every time the sacrament of baptism is administered and a new born child of God comes forth from the font pure and immaculate in baptismal innocence. Thus, just as the Church is born pure and undefiled in the sacrament, so too was Mary born immaculate in her physical person. And both Mary and the Church are born in imitation of the most unique and immaculately pure birth of all: the birth of Jesus Christ.

The assumption of Mary provides yet another illustration of the Church's singular veneration of the virgin. Forty days after Easter Jesus ascended into heaven. This he was perfectly able to do "under his own power" because he is God. Mary followed in the path of her son. Unlike Christ she did not rise into heaven by her own power. Rather, mere creature that she is, she was taken up by God; "assumed." While the Church has never defined that Mary died (or did not die) it seems only proper and to be expected that her imitation of her divine son would include death. Then immediately thereafter, before her body which had borne the savior could undergo the corruption of the grave, she was taken up into heaven in a manner less radical than Jesus, who had spent forty risen days among his fellow men before the day of his ascension.

We too, members of the Church of Jesus Christ, believe in the resurrection of the body. Christ's resurrection and ascension were the most perfect, then less perfectly was the assumption of Mary, and finally comes our own bodily resurrection at the end of the world. Thus the birth of the Church and her final destiny are mirrored first and most perfectly in Jesus Christ. Then in a manner superior to us, though inferior to Christ, is our birth and destiny as the Church reflected in Mary, mother of God.

Between the immaculate conception and the assumption

there is a close relationship and one in which the Church takes great pride as well as inspiration. The Church, the fruit of the redemption, is perfectly represented by the handmaid of the lord who cooperated so well in carrying out the mission of Easter.

The oldest independent marian feast is the feast of the assumption. While this feast appears in the Roman liturgy only as late as the seventh century it is actually much older. In the orient of the fourth and fifth centuries it was commemorated by the Nestorians and Monophysites, whose calendars have been preserved, and of course there is the fourth century Church of the Dormition in Jerusalem. Dormition is the ancient name for the feast of the assumption. Literally it means the sleeping of Mary prior to her being taken up into heaven.

The feast of the annunciation is obviously later than the feast of Christmas for its date (March 25) is dependent on Dec 25 for its meaning. In fact this feast was originally a feast of Jesus known as the feast of the annunciation of the lord. It appeared in the Roman calendar sometime between the fifth and seventh centuries. Somewhat later there appeared the feast of the immaculate conception. While this feast first appeared in Italy in the ninth century it was not until the latter part of the sixteenth century that it was extended to the whole Church by Pius V.

One of the most interesting marian feasts and the one that we perhaps hear least about is the purification of Mary, Feb 2. This ancient feast, which comes forty days after Christmas, is actually the close of the Christmas season although it sometimes happens that it comes after Septuagesima Sunday. This tradition lives on today in many parts of Europe where cribs and Christmas decorations are left up until Feb 2. The idea of a feast on the fortieth day after Christmas goes back to the Church in Jerusalem, where it was celebrated at least as early as the fourth century. The modern name for the feast, the purification, is semitic in origin and reflects its Jewish background. The Greeks on the other hand chose to see in the feast the entrance of Jesus into the temple and his meeting with Simeon. The name of the feast in Greek is still hypapante, which literally means meeting.

The procession during the feast of the purification is also oriental in origin, but it was not introduced in Rome until the seventh century when, like so many things in our liturgy, it was instituted as a countermeasure to a pagan procession of atonement. This fact accounts for the purple vestments. The carrying of lights is at least as old as the eighth century, and of course the receiving of the candle from the priest signifies the share in the life of Christ (sanctifying grace) which has but one divine source. While the prayers and canticles at the blessing of the candles are also ancient they betray the medieval tendency to obscure the procession with lengthy blessings and prayers.

The Church has thus surrounded the veneration of Mary with a rich and meaningful liturgy. Since the spirit of the liturgy is the spirit of the Church it is here that our devotion to the mother of God should take its leitmotif. The formulations of the prayers in the masses of our lady give us a fine insight into the Church's teaching on her.

We have attempted to show in our consideration of the Christmas season that the Church is presenting the coming of the redeemer according to her teaching on the person of the God-man. The divine aspect is the theme of the feast of the Epiphany. This theme is clearly echoed in the Sundays after Epiphany. At Christmas the liturgy stresses the human aspect, the savior's birth, whereby Jesus became a man, a member of Adam's family, one of us. The theme is continued in the feasts of Mary, his mother.

Having thus considered the redeemer's coming and person, we can now turn to his work.

## 3

## THE REDEEMER'S WORK

### The Prelenten Season

We have noted that the center of Christian life and worship is Easter. The Easter season is the most solemn and the most ancient time of the Church year. Not only is Easter itself preceded by a forty day period, but even this preparatory time is preceded by three weeks during which we "prepare to prepare." So solemn and so serious does the Church consider the lenten time that she would not have us enter into it without adequate preparation. The three Sundays of this pre-preparatory season, Septuagesima, Sexagesima and Quinquagesima, are a sort of vestibule to lent. They are both preparation and transition. For the Church begins now to direct us toward Christ's work, which is the theme of the Easter time.

The official names for these three Sundays, literally seventy, sixty and fifty respectively, do not indicate precisely those numbers of days before Easter—only Quinquagesima Sunday is literally exact. Rather the names mean the "Sunday within the seventy day period" before Easter, etc. Thus the Latin term is not Dominica Septuagesima but rather

Dominica in Septuagesima, and so forth. The same is true for the Sundays in Lent.

The three prelenten Sundays were eastern in origin and were introduced in Rome in the sixth century ostensibly as days of prayer during the time of the Lombard invasions. Many of the prayers in the missal which beg God's protection date from this period—some by Gregory the Great. A number of the prayers said on these Sundays seem to reflect the urgency of the time.

Among the liturgical variations encountered on Septuagesima are the use of purple vestments and the omission of the alleluia. The Te Deum and the gloria are also omitted. From the ninth century onward the departure of the alleluia from the liturgy was often commemorated by a special office. This custom is still apparent in the office today by the twofold alleluia added to the benedicamus domino of vespers on the Saturday before Septuagesima Sunday. Interestingly enough this medieval custom of "burying the alleluia" is not unknown in the United States today. In Worship[1] Martin B. Hellriegel, pastor of Holy Cross Parish in St Louis and a pioneer of the American liturgical movement, has related how the alleluia is "buried" in his parish each year at this time. The service he uses is simple, moving and meaningful.

In everyday language then the prelenten season is the time when we stop to get our bearings: we look backward to see who it is who has come to be our redeemer, and we look ahead to see what we must do to follow him.

[1] See Worship XXX, 3, Feb 1956, 206.

## The Lenten Season

The history of lent is a long and involved one. Much of it is of interest chiefly to those who are engaged in liturgical science; for this reason we will confine ourselves only to those aspects of lent which might increase our understanding of it as we know it today.

In the fourth century the idea of a forty day period of preparation for Easter began to take hold. The number forty was chosen mainly because Jesus had fasted forty days and forty nights, and the lenten season was to be a period of prayer, more intense religious life, and fasting. In the beginning however lent and fasting were not as synonymous as they are today. Lent began with what we still call the first Sunday of lent, and the secret of that mass still refers to the beginning of the lenten season. And the official name for lent is Quadragesima, or the forty day period.

It might be asked though how the fourth century Christian community reckoned forty days from the first Sunday in lent until Easter. If there are six weeks in lent, and seven days in a week, one would expect forty-two days in lent. But in those days lent ended with Holy Thursday and the Easter celebration began on Good Friday. Easter to the early Christians was not so much the event of Christ's death and resurrection as it was the celebration of the redemption—which is the real meaning of Christ's death and resurrection taken together. Thus there were only five days of lent in holy week (Palm Sunday to Holy Thursday), leaving five other weeks in lent, or thirty-five days. The thirty-five days from the first Sunday of lent to the end of passion week, plus the five days of holy week, equals forty days.

Later on however, during the sixth and seventh centuries, new factors entered in which altered the lenten season somewhat. In the first place fasting was becoming ever more the central theme of the lenten observance. Secondly the closing of lent came to be considered not Holy Thursday midnight, but the midnight of Holy Saturday. In addition, since earliest times, no one fasted on Sundays since Sunday was always dominated by the resurrection theme. Thus the Sundays of lent could not be counted as fast days. And since there are six Sundays in lent, six minus forty two leaves thirty six days remaining in lent.

While this arrangment seemed suitable to some (notably John Cassian, who saw in the number thirty six a tenth of the year, and thus a tithing of the days of the year to God in fast), to others it was imperfect because there had to be forty days of fasting according to the example of Christ. Obviously the only solution lay in adding four days to the thirty six days of fast. Thus the beginning of lent was pushed back past the first Sunday of lent to the Wednesday before, that is to say, to what is now called Ash Wednesday. So the Church can now call the period between Ash Wednesday and Easter Sunday "the forty day period," even though by actual count there are forty six days in lent.

Originally the Wednesday ashes were distributed only to those who were to do public penance during lent, but in time the conferring of ashes was extended to everyone as a sign of the humility and penance we should possess as we embark upon the holy season, and as we prepare ourselves for the "solemnity of solemnities" which lies ahead.

## The First Week of Lent

The liturgy of any feast or season of the liturgical year necessarily provides important clues to the meaning and purpose of the celebration itself. It is only logical that in the liturgy of Christmas the gospel of the birth of Jesus Christ is read, or that on the feast of the annunciation we read about the coming of the angel Gabriel to the virgin Mary. Following this principle the lenten masses yield a wealth of information about the meaning of the holy season.

There are three main themes which find expression in the masses of lent: penance, preparation for baptism, and of course the passion of Jesus.

The penance theme begins with the bestowing of ashes on the penitents on Ash Wednesday and dominates the liturgy up until the second Sunday of lent. Reference is of course made throughout lent in the collects of the masses to fasting, etc. but it is primarily during the first week that the compilers of the missal intended to stress this theme of penance.

In earlier times it was the custom during lent for public penance to be carried out by those who were in need of it—and everyone was supposed to do public penance for his or her sins at least once. And since lent began on the first Sunday of lent, and since no one did penance on Sunday, the actual public penance and the liturgical rites which surrounded it began on the Monday of the first week of lent. Thus we have the reading from Ezechiel on God judging his flock, and the gospel of the second coming of Jesus as judge and his separation of the good from the bad. This latter thought is especially pertinent if we recall that those who were doing penance were given their own place in church, in a place separate from the rest of the congregation.

Another custom, somewhat later in origin, was the driving of the penitents out of the church by the bishop, just as God had driven Adam and Eve, the original sinners, out of paradise. This theme is expressed on Tuesday of the first week of lent, when the gospel text concerns Jesus driving the money changers out of the temple. To this day many of the old cathedrals of Europe have their "Adam's door" decorated with scenes of God driving our first parents out of the garden. It was through this door that the bishop drove the public penitents. Moreover, since many sinners were thought to be possessed by the devil, the gospel of Wednesday of the first week deals with possession by devils. In Thursday's gospel Jesus tells us that he has been sent to the lost sheep of the house of Israel.

## The Second and Third Weeks

While the second week of lent has no special theme as such, in the third week the preparation for baptism permeates the lenten liturgy. In the early Christian community all candidates for baptism were exorcised several times before receiving the sacrament. In the gospel for the third Sunday of lent we hear of this subject. On Monday of the third week, the story of the cleansing of Namaan the Syrian depicts baptism as a cleansing from sin. Since during those days the instruction of the candidates was intensified, the gospels for the week concern such subjects as the authority of the Church (Tuesday) and the sin of hypocrisy (Wednesday). References are also made to Jesus' miracles of cleansing and healing, and to Aaron's making the water flow from the rock to satiate the Israelites—the rock referring to Jesus and the water to the baptismal waters.

On the same day (Friday of the third week) there is another reference to baptism, the story of Jesus and the Samaritan woman. In the story of Susanna Saturday's epistle tells of the suffering of the just—again a reference to Jesus. The gospel warns of the sinfulness of adultery.

## The Fourth Week

Wednesday of the fourth week was an ancient fast day in the Roman liturgy. It was a day of special instruction for those who were preparing for baptism on Holy Saturday night during the Easter vigil. The introit from Ezechiel and the readings bear witness to this. The gospel of the man born blind who receives his sight refers to the fact that baptism is enlightenment, which was an early name for this sacrament. Those who were baptized were the enlightened. The ancient character of this day is also pointed up by the fact that there are three readings instead of the usual two—the presence of three readings usually indicating the antiquity of a mass text. Another interesting feature of the fourth week and one which also points up its antiquity is the fact that it was on Saturday that ordinations to the priesthood were held in the early Roman Church. The mass celebrated on Passion Sunday was originally part of the vigil service which began on Saturday night and culminated in the morning. The epistle and the communion verse still refer to the priesthood of Christ and its institution. The ember days were also times of ordination, at least since the fifth century. This custom has not died out entirely, and in some places in Europe ordinations are still held either on this Saturday or on Passion Sunday itself.

In the early days of the development of lent in Rome there were three weeks of fasting prior to Easter. This was the first lent. The first week began with what is now known as Laetare Sunday, the fourth Sunday of lent. Passion Sunday was therefore the second Sunday or the middle Sunday of the three that preceded Easter—Palm Sunday being the third. Thus Passion Sunday was formerly known as the middle Sunday or Dominica mediana.

In the late fifth century Pope Gelasius titled the week which preceded Passion Sunday the middle week or hebdomada mediana. The week got its name not from the calendar position as the middle week but from the fact that it preceded the Sunday called Dominica mediana. That the Sunday should receive its name from the preceding and not the following week is explained when we recall that Sunday was long considered the eighth day of the week, and not the first. It was not until after Pope Gelasius that the whole question of having forty fast days became prominent and the development which we have already described began.

The mass on the Saturday before Passion Sunday also refers to baptism and was originally intended (at least as far as the texts are concerned) for catechumens. This formula also appears to be very ancient. This mass may have been a special one for the catechumens, who were not permitted to attend the ordination mass at the night vigil. Or perhaps the text of the ordination mass was transferred to Sunday and this one put in its place on Saturday morning, when ordinations became more popular at other times.

## The Fifth Week

The fifth week of lent, which is the first week of passiontide, concentrates wholly on the passion of Jesus. This is evidenced in both the mass and the divine office.

On Passion Sunday, for the first time during lent, the statues in all the churches are veiled. A number of explanations are put forward for this practice, but the simplest seems to be the medieval custom of hanging a veil in front of the sanctuary, thus cutting it off from the view of the congregation. This would have been an easy task especially in those churches which had a rood screen, as in England. The reasoning behind this custom may have been that during this time of penance the faithful should deprive themselves even of the sight of the holy place in the church. Another explanation is that the veiling is an allusion to the words "Jesus hid himself and went out of the temple" in the gospel of the day. In medieval times this veil was hung at the very beginning of lent. As the architecture of churches changed in the course of time it was found necessary to veil the statues individually. The time of the veiling was probably changed to Passion Sunday to accentuate this time as one of even greater penance as Easter drew nearer.

Also noticeable for the first time on Passion Sunday is the absence of the prayers at the foot of the altar and the "Glory be to the father, etc." at the end of the psalms. As is the case with many peculiarities of the lenten liturgy—as we will soon see—these prayers were simply not added to the liturgy at this time of the year. In other words when the prayers at the foot of the altar were added to the mass and the doxology to the end of the psalms, they were added at all times of the year except at this time. Thus what is today considered an omission is in reality a "nonaddition."

The readings of the masses of passion week refer in part to the coming sufferings of the savior (Old Testament readings) and set the stage for the events of Jesus' passion (gospels). During this time Jesus the lord speaks ever more insistently to the world both about his divinity and his mission; at the same time he foretells the events of the coming week.

On Monday we read the beautiful gospel from the seventh chapter of John in which Jesus refers to the fountains of living water—a reference, as the evangelist explains, to the Spirit which would be given those who believe in him. Scholars have pointed out that the true meaning of Jn 7:38 is that the living waters will flow from the side of Jesus Christ, not from the person who believes in him. The picture Jesus is presenting to us is one of himself, with grace pouring out from within him to sanctify mankind. As John later tells us, there did indeed flow from the side of the savior a stream of water as he hung upon the cross, his side pierced in death.

The Tuesday epistle tells the story of Daniel in the lion's den—a reference to the manner in which Jesus will be saved from his sufferings by the resurrection. As Daniel came up from the pit so too would Jesus emerge from the grave.

The reading on the law, taken from Leviticus, was Wednesday's instruction for the catechumens. In the gospel Jesus asserts that he and his father are one. On Thursday Jesus tells us that the more we need forgiveness the greater is his love for us. This passage is especially meaningful because his hour approaches.

## Holy Week

One of the basic principles of modern liturgical science was formulated by the late German lay scholar Anton Baumstark, and it can be summarized as follows: the oldest liturgical traditions are preserved in the feasts of highest liturgical rank. Since for over three hundred years the Church celebrated no feast other than Easter it is not surprising, upon applying Baumstark's principle, to find the Easter celebration filled with practices which go back to the earliest days of the Church.

Still another key to the understanding of the Easter

celebration is the fact that since the earliest liturgy was celebrated in Jerusalem and environs, it was only natural that the various services should be closely associated with the places where the actual events of Easter took place and even with the times when they occurred. Thus we have an evening mass on Holy Thursday, a service on Good Friday afternoon, etc. But nowhere is this tendency more in evidence than on Palm Sunday, when as early as the fourth century a palm procession was held from Mount Olivet into the city of Jerusalem in such wise that the original event was imitated as closely as possible.

This Palm Sunday precession soon came to the west, among the Franks at first, and was surrounded with great solemnity and drama. Usually a cross, a gospel book or some other representation of Jesus was carried in the procession, which would often stop at the entrance to the city, where the homage of the citizens was made. As early as the seventh century the palms were blessed with a special blessing. In time new elements were added, such as a wooden donkey on wheels with a statue or figure of Jesus mounted on it. It was only inevitable that the carrying of the blessed sacrament should be introduced.

Not until the ninth and tenth centuries did the rite of blessing the palms begin to take on such proportions that it all but obscured the procession. Since 1955 the blessings have been curtailed so that the procession in honor of Christ the king is once again the central act.

The ancient traditions we have already referred to are especially evident during the sacred triduum of Jesus' death, burial and resurrection, since these three days have formed the heart of the Easter celebration since apostolic times. The most meaningful and ancient tradition of all is the custom whereby the Church does not celebrate mass on Good Friday and Holy Saturday, but only after midnight of Holy Saturday, in the early hours of Easter Sunday. This illustrates how the Church values the great unity of the Easter mystery. In this one paschal mass the Church sacramentally celebrates the sacred events of these three days. It is also the custom during these days to forbid the private celebration of mass, and in this prohibition the ancient tradition of concelebration is preserved.

The rubrics for Holy Thursday and the following days recommend that other available priests be present for the one service. At the ordination of a priest the newly ordained actually consecrates the host and chalice with the bishop, but this is a later form: the ancient tradition is still practiced at Easter.

On Holy Thursday at the evening mass, the restored holy week rite directs, if there is a tabernacle on the main altar it should be empty. All the hosts for the congregation must be consecrated at the evening mass. In former times the people brought the bread which was to be used at the mass, a custom Pius XII recommended in his liturgical encyclical *Mediator Dei.*

Another interesting custom on Holy Thursday is the stripping of the altar of all linens and other ornaments. This was always done after these services had ended; only when the altar was to be used were linens and ornaments placed upon it. During the middle ages the custom arose of making this very stripping a rite in itself, accompanied by psalms. Today this ancient practice survives only on these last three days of holy week.

## Good Friday

The Good Friday liturgy contains a number of interesting features. First there is the prostration before the altar at the beginning of the service. This ancient custom, which survives only once a year in this form, is really a forerunner of our present confiteor. It was during this prostration that the pope or bishop made a silent confession of his sins.

The Good Friday liturgy also contains many ancient congregational devotions: scripture readings, prayers and songs. It might be noted that the present foremass derives from these early congregational devotions. When the early Christians gathered together for a noneucharistic service they did what is still done on Good Friday—without of course the veneration of the cross or communion.

The prayers for Good Friday were a part of every service in the early centuries of the Church; although they were eventually discontinued in other services they were retained on Good Friday because of the dignity and antiquity of the day. But these prayers are interesting for a reason in addition to their antiquity—in substance they go back to the first century—namely because they show clearly the early form of Christian prayer. First there is an introduction to the prayer which states what it is the congregation will pray for. As an example, the congregation is first asked to pray for the holy Church of God. Then the individual members of the congregation are asked to kneel and offer silent prayers for the Church. Then everyone is asked to stand so that all of the private individual petitions may be gathered together by the priest and offered to God in the collect. This example shows clearly what the Roman liturgy did and does allow for the private and silent prayers of the individual.

The veneration of the cross is an eastern devotion which was very popular in Syria and which in the eighth century became a part of the western liturgy. It was an instance of a popular devotion which became part of what is now the official liturgy of the Church. In those days there was no legislative distinction between types of services, so the transition was not what it would be today. But it is also an illustration of how the liturgy was itself the "devotion" of the people.

The reception of holy communion on Good Friday is a revival of what was at one time a popular custom in both Rome and in the north. Prior to the fifth century there was no communion anywhere on Good Friday. As time went on certain developments necessitated a change. In the north Holy Thursday was the day on which those who were doing public penance were reconciled to the Church. It was on Holy Thursday that they received the long awaited absolution. Only natural then was their desire to receive holy communion as soon as possible after their reconciliation. Thus it came about that the penitents were permitted to receive on Good Friday, which for a time even developed into a popular communion day.

In Rome the Good Friday communion was introduced for different reasons. We have already traced the development whereby Good Friday and Holy Saturday became fast days in lent rather than the first part of the Easter celebration. But in the seventh century the custom had arisen of receiving holy communion every day during lent. Therefore the people wanted to receive on Good Friday as well. Reception on Saturday presented no problem since the Easter vigil was already being pushed back. The so-called mass of the presanctified was introduced on Good Friday as the communion service for the people. In the ninth century the papal liturgy reverted to the older practice somewhat when it restricted the reception of communion to the celebrant alone.

From what we have said thus far it should be clear that the Easter vigil service is the principle service of the Church year. This service more than any other gives the Church year its true meaning. Everything which has gone before it has been a preparation for it, and everything that comes after it continues to echo and explain it. The Easter vigil is, in the words of Augustine, the "mother of vigils."

## The Easter Vigil

All the principle themes of Easter are clearly expressed in this venerable Easter "rite." First there is the blessing of the fire and the lighting of the candle, which is perhaps the most ancient illustration used to explain the work of Christ, who passed through darkness to light. There is also the lighting of candles by the congregation with the light which has derived from the one paschal candle that represents Jesus. Then the deacon sings the hymn in praise of the redemption, the Exsultet. From this magnificent hymn it becomes clear that this night of the year is truly the holy

night, the night of nights. The deacon sings of the true
lamb offered for our sins. He reminds us of the first passover, when the children of Israel passed dry shod through
the Red Sea, and he proclaims that this is the night when
Christ burst the bonds of death and arose victorious from
the grave. It is on this night that the Church calls the sin of
Adam the "happy fault" because it required the redeemer.
And we are reminded that on this night heaven is united to
earth, divinity is joined with humanity.

In the readings from the Old Testament the liturgy tells
us how God prepared the world for the coming of Christ,
and above all for this night. After the first part of the litany
has been invoked the liturgy turns to baptism. In the
solemn prayer of the blessings of the waters the whole
theology of baptism and redemption is masterfully presented. The Church prays that God will make the waters
fertile for regeneration by Christ and his bride the Church
in holy baptism. The prayer recalls how the Spirit of the
lord first moved over the waters, and then begs God to
multiply his saving act of regeneration within these waters.
And it goes on to beg for a heavenly offspring conceived in
holiness, coming forth from the spotless womb of the baptismal font. The paschal candle is plunged into the waters
to symbolize the mystical union between Christ and his
people from which the power of the Holy Spirit goes
forth. Following the blessing of the waters the sacrament
of baptism itself is administered. After the conclusion of
the litany the great moment comes, and the paschal eucharist, the most solemn and meaningful mass of the year, is
offered. Already it is in the early hours of Sunday, the great
resurrection day. In this mass the actual redemption itself

is realized and we ourselves partake in the very core of Jesus' work in our behalf. This is Easter.

During the Easter vigil mass there is no offertory or communion verse. This is a sign of the greatest antiquity, especially in the case of the communion hymn, the oldest hymn in the Roman mass.

It is a pity that this most solemn and venerable of all worship services is often looked upon simply as a midnight mass which the faithful may attend simply to fulfill their obligations. It is unfortunate that the preceding service is often considered merely a series of blessings, trivial sacramentals which should be gotten over with as simply, and as quickly, as possible.

### The Easter Mystery

The Christian religion is basically an Easter religion. The whole Christian faith is based on Easter—"If Christ be not risen, our faith is in vain," says Paul. The holy sacrifice of the mass is a celebration of Easter regardless of the time of year. The Church prays through Jesus Christ "who lives and reigns forever." The question then is: what is Easter? For Easter is not only the event of Christ's resurrection. Only the passion and resurrection taken together give meaning to the feast—that is to say, Easter is the celebration of man's redemption. This, and not merely the event of the first Easter, must be the theme of our discussion here.

A careful examination of the liturgy of holy week reveals that there is in fact a three day celebration of the one mystery of redemption. Since the earliest days the sacred triduum of the crucifixion, burial and resurrection has formed the heart of the liturgy. Even as early as the fourth century Augustine makes this very clear.

Holy Thursday is a sort of vestibule to these three sacred days. In truth, Holy Thursday derives its whole meaning from Good Friday and Easter Sunday.

The mystery of redemption has two phases: the death and resurrection of Jesus. By his passage through the death of the cross to the life of resurrection Jesus fulfilled the plan of God the father for the redemption of the world. Therefore these two phases of the one redemption must be taken together to be properly understood. The one is meaningless without the other.

The holy week liturgy shows how the Church celebrates the redemption. For no mass is celebrated on Good Friday. During the three sacred days, Friday, Saturday and Sunday, mass is celebrated only once—after midnight of Holy Saturday, in the early hours of Easter Sunday morning. This one mass, which is the climax of the Easter vigil service, celebrates the events of these three days. Since in every mass the death and resurrection of Jesus are present, only one mass is required to realize these two events which together are redemption.

Good Friday is in a way a "prayers at the foot of the altar" to the mass of the Easter vigil. Holy Saturday might be called its offertory. The Easter vigil mass bears this out for the preface sings of "the true paschal lamb who took away the sins of the world" (Good Friday), "who by dying destroyed our death" (Good Friday), and who by rising restored our life (Easter Sunday). Conversely on Good Friday the Church praises the resurrection in the midst of her mourning and sings of the now glorious cross adorned

with the purple of the king. And even on Good Friday
the Church prays through Jesus Christ who lives and
reigns forever. Thus the death and resurrection of Jesus are
not two separate events on the Church calendar but rather
the two phases of the mystery of redemption. Good Friday
through Easter is truly the passover of the lord.

Another indication of the meaning of these three days is
the administration of baptism at the Easter vigil, for in
baptism redemption is worked on us first and most radically.
Baptism is also a passage from death to life. "Do you not
know that as many of us as were baptized into Jesus Christ
were baptized into his death? Therefore we were buried
with him by baptism into death that as Christ was raised
up from the dead by the glory of his father so also we
should walk in the newness of life. For if we have been
united with him in the likeness of his death, we shall also
be in the likeness of his resurrection" (Paul to the Romans,
6:6). Baptism is therefore the Easter sacrament.

Easter then really embraces three days: Good Friday,
Holy Saturday and Easter Sunday. Still another manner of
indicating the nature of Easter is to point out the origin
of these three days, although it is impossible to determine
precisely when each day came to be observed. Certainly the
original celebration took place on Easter Sunday morning.
At this service, among other things, the whole account of
the passion and resurrection of Jesus was read. Presumably
this was still the case in the early fifth century, for one
writer tells us that on Sundays in Jerusalem, as the "gospel
of the resurrection" was read, there was great wailing and
lamentation. The gospel of the resurrection obviously included the crucifixion.

It could not have been long however before that portion of the gospel dealing with the passion and death was transferred from Sunday back to Friday and read on that day as well, for it was only natural that the more sorrowful parts of the Easter service take place on the day of Jesus' death. When this was done, or what the exact contents of the original service were, cannot be ascertained. The important thing to remember is that Good Friday is simply the first part of Easter Sunday. This fact is borne out both theologically and historically.

## Eastertide

The paschaltide is of course characterized by the resurrection theme. The abundance of alleluias and the joyful character of the introits of the Sundays after Easter, as well as the Easter preface used during this time, bear witness to Easter's joy. The gospel of the good shepherd on the second Sunday after Easter also accentuates the resurrection theme.

As we noted above the liturgy has a tendency to look ahead, and this is especially evident in the gospels of the third, fourth and fifth Sundays after Easter. In fact these gospels are already looking forward to the ascension and to Pentecost. The reason for this anticipation is perhaps more theological than liturgical. In our discussion of the meaning of Easter we saw that the death and resurrection of Jesus Christ are not two unrelated events on the Church calendar, but rather the component parts of the core in the mystery of redemption. Even so God's plan for our redemption did not stop with Jesus' resurrection. There were other phases of this same central mystery of faith which Jesus was to fulfill before assuming his place at the right hand of the father. The first of these is the ascension, the second is Pentecost. These two feasts are also integrally bound up with the paschal mystery.

It was God's plan that mankind should have a "mediator between God and man, himself man, Christ Jesus," who would be "constantly interceding for us" as our "advocate with the father." This is why the Church prays through Jesus Christ "who lives and reigns forever." This mediatorship is the work of the risen one, and it is also the meaning of the feast of the ascension. The resurrection was significant and meaningful for man because by it Jesus today sits at the right hand of his father, "constantly interceding for us." And in order that man might not be destitute, in order that he might still have the consolation of his abiding presence, Jesus sent his Holy Spirit to dwell among us until the end of the world. It is the presence of his Spirit which gives life and vigor to the Church and renders her eternally young and fresh, which keeps her from error, which make her holy. With the descent of the Holy Spirit Jesus' work of redemption was completed for now; its final completion will of course be realized at his second coming.

In the gospel for the third Sunday after Easter Jesus tells his disciples: "A little while, and now you shall not see me; and again a little while, and you shall see me; because I go to the father." To these words the Church adds a twofold alleluia in the communion verse. Even though his going means that we will no longer see him physically in this world we will see him in the next, and in the meantime we will enjoy the abiding presence of his Holy Spirit. Any sorrow we experience now will be transformed into a joy that no one can take from us.

On the fourth Sunday after Easter Jesus tells us that "I go to him that sent me." He tells us that it is better for us if he goes, "for if I go not, the Paraclete will not come to you, but if I go, I will send him to you. . . . He shall glorify me, because he shares in what is mine, and he shall proclaim it to you." Here again the liturgy looks forward to Jesus' going in body and his coming in spirit.

On the fifth Sunday, the Sunday before the ascension, Jesus tells us to ask his father for anything in his name. Since by the ascension Jesus becomes to some extent visibly the meditaor, it is only natural that we should think of him as the one through whom we pray. The rogation days which occur during this final week of the ascension point up this mediatorial role of our lord. Rogation days are literally "asking days." And because of the oneness and organic unity of the work of the redemption the Church sees nothing incongruous in speaking of the two phases, ascension and Pentecost, during the time of the resurrection—just as on Good Friday she refers to Easter Sunday, and on Easter Sunday to Good Friday.

## Rogation Days

### LITANIES MINOR AND MAJOR

On Monday, Tuesday and Wednesday of the week of the ascension occur what are known as rogation days, or minor litanies. These three days are called minor in comparison with the litany of April 25, the feast of Mark the evangelist, which is called the major litany. This distinction between major and minor is rooted solely in the fact that the use of the April 25 litany is more ancient than that of the three days before the feast of the ascension.

The litany invoked on all four days is exactly the same. The major litany however is still another instance of the christianizing of a pagan festival: the twenty-fifth day of April had been the pagan feast day of the god Robigo, who was invoked to ward off late frosts that could ruin the crops. Exactly when this ancient festival was converted by the Church to a Christian feast is not known. Although it is first mentioned by Gregory the Great there can be little doubt that it is much more ancient. It was probably an established custom by his time.

Since the ancient pagan festival had also had a procession, so too did the Christians. The route followed by the Christians was similar to the one formerly used by the pagans except that it veered off to a station church. Stops were made at the Milvian Bridge, at a cross somewhere along the way, and finally at St Peter's Basilica. The prayers recited at each of these stops along the way are found in the Gregorian sacramentary which Hadrian I sent to Charlemagne.

The minor litanies preceding the feast of the ascension are gallic in origin. They were first introduced by Bishop Manmertus of Vienna in 470 at a time of great distress in his area. Later, in 511, three days were extended to all the frankish realm by the Council of Orleans, which termed them "rogationes id est litanieas." Thus the term rogation or asking day, from the Latin rogare, to ask. These minor litanies were not introduced in Rome until the time of Leo III, which would have been around 800. These days also have a pagan precedent in Rome. Originally there had been three consecutive days in May during which processions were held, again for agricultural reasons, and in time they had come to be associated with the magically effected expulsion of evil spirits from the environs of the city. The rogation days were a logical countermeasure, and thus the entire rite was christianized. The obvious reason for placing these days immediately before the feast of the ascension is to emphasize the mediatorial role of Jesus.

These minor litanies underwent some revision in 1961 when the new rubrics were promulgated. For one thing ordinaries were granted the right to change the observance of these days to another time of the year which might be more meaningful to the faithful whose agricultural time-table might not coincide with that of ancient Rome. Also the obligation to recite the litanies in the divine office was lifted. These three days before the ascension can still be meaningful if employed as a triduum in honor of Jesus, mediator to God for all men.


## Ascension: Feast of Jesus the Mediator

The feast of our lord's ascension is what might be called the next to last step in the Easter cycle. Like Pentecost, which follows ten days later, it is not a celebration unto itself but rather another aspect of the mystery of the redemption. It too is a part of Easter.

As with any feast in the Church year we must always distinguish between the event being celebrated and the meaning of the event in God's redemptive plan. In this instance the historical event itself, the actual going up into heaven by Jesus, is celebrated. But the real meaning of the event is expressed every time the Church addresses a prayer to God the father through Jesus Christ "who lives and reigns forever." Every time she recites this formula the Church is expressing her constant and abiding Easter existence. As we saw above in our discussion of the rogation days, it is the mediatorship of Christ that the ascension brings before us. For the Christ who ascended is of course the risen Easter Christ through whom, as he told us, all men come to the father.

In his first epistle to Timothy the apostle tells us that "there is one God, and one mediator, himself man, Christ Jesus, who gave himself a ransom for all" (2:5–6). These words contain the meaning of the feast of the ascension. We already know that there is but one God and that Jesus is the one bridge between him and man. But it is interesting to note that in referring to Jesus as mediator Paul is saying that it is as man that he is exercising this function. Jesus' mediatorship is provided by God entirely for man's benefit, not for his own. And although it is true that God used the humanity of his son to become one of us and to reimpress his image upon us, this action too was exclusively for our sake. Thus it is through Jesus the man that we have our access to God, through Jesus the man that our interests are represented in heaven, through Jesus the man as its head that humanity stands before its creator. To Paul the fact that God's chosen representative should not only be his son but a man as well was something awesome, for he found in the ascension the greatest consolation and a truth which brought with it a real sense of closeness to God. This is a

striking aspect of the Easter mystery. We are in Jesus and
he is with God. This man who actually rose from the dead
and went ahead of us to heaven is truly in God's most im-
mediate and intimate presence—and he is inseparable from
us! Whatever we ask the father in his name will be granted.


## Pentecost

The term Pentecost is a Greek equivalent for the Latin
words which we have already noted such as Septuagesima,
Sexigesima, etc. (seventy day, sixty day). It means the
*fifticth* day after Easter. There is nothing in the word
Pentecost which designates the Holy Spirit.

The feast of Pentecost, like all feasts of the Church year,
is observed solely because it celebrates something which is
an integral part of the mystery of the redemption, that is to
say, of Easter. Pentecost concludes that part of the Church
year which is concerned directly with the work Jesus came
to perform. Christmas and the Epiphany are more concerned with the person of the redeemer.

The question then is how Pentecost fits into the frame-
work of the redemption. To begin with we might recall
Jesus' words that he will be with us "even to the end of the
world." We might also recall that he said it was better for
him to leave us so that the Holy Spirit could dwell with us.
This Spirit would be a recipient "of what is mine" and
would bear witness concerning Jesus to the Church. And
this same Spirit, the creed tells us, "proceeds from the father
and the son." Thus, ten days later on the Sunday called
Pentecost, having ascended bodily into heaven on Ascen-

sion Thursday, Jesus the lord returns to his people, to the Church, by means of the Holy Spirit.

The Holy Spirit, third person of the trinity, is the Spirit of Christ, now present in us, his Church, as the source of our divine life and as the principle which binds together the new people of God. The Church testifies to this truth in every mass and office when she prays "through Jesus Christ who lives and reigns in the unity of the Holy Spirit." This "unity of the Holy Spirit" is nothing other than the Church herself, that is to say, the people of God in whom the Spirit dwells and by means of whom Christ "lives and reigns" in this world. Thus the feast of Pentecost marks the completion of the first phase of the work of the redemption. The final stage will be at the parousia, the final coming of Jesus Christ at the end of the world.

Pentecost then is the savior's way of continuing in time and space the work Jesus came to do in Palestine two thousand years ago. The work is continued through the ministry of his Church, in which he dwells by his Holy Spirit, and in whom he will live and reign forever.

### Trinity Sunday

The feast of the most holy trinity, which follows Pentecost Sunday, might be called a summary of all that has happened since the Church began to celebrate the mystery of Jesus Christ at Christmas time. All that has happened in the process of effecting man's salvation, from Christmas through Easter and Pentecost, has been the result of the saving activity of the three persons of the trinity.

The idea of a feast in honor of the three pesons of the

trinity resulted from the anti-Arian struggles in the north of Europe around the time of the eighth century. The emphasis on the divinity of Christ and his place as the second divine person naturally led to an emphasis on the trinity itself. Whereas in earlier times Jesus was considered more under the aspect of his victorious and glorified humanity, the denial by Arius, the Alexandrian priest, of his divinity prompted the Church to stress the fact that Jesus is God. The old manner of praising God through the son in the Holy Spirit gave way to praising the father and the son and the Holy Spirit.

In time, although with some difficulty, the new stress was incorporated in the public prayers of the Church. Alcuin, the deacon who was Charlemagne's liturgist, composed a mass in honor of the trinity for use on Sundays, and this mass soon came to be associated with the first Sunday after Pentecost. The first reference to an actual feast of the holy trinity was in Liege in 920. However Alexander II felt that the trinity was honored every day of the year in the canon of the mass and that a special feast was unnecessary. Not until the twentieth century, in 1911, was the feast given the highest then-existing rank: double of the first class.

The trinitarian text which is perhaps best known is the preface of the feast of the most holy trinity; it is also called the Sunday preface because of its use on most Sundays of the year. This preface is a product of the late sixth or early seventh century and comes from Spain. It was not until 1759 that this preface became the Sunday preface as we know it. It is not unlikely that the Second Vatican Council will give us a Sunday preface more in keeping with the Easter character of the day.

## 4

Easter Applied

*Corpus Christi*

As Jungmann has so aptly put it, the feast of the sacred heart, which falls on a Friday, is a sort of Good Friday seen from within. This same idea holds true for the feast of Corpus Christi, which is always celebrated on a Thursday and which is an outgrowth of Holy Thursday. It is an outgrowth in the sense that the theme of both days is the same, only on Corpus Christi there is opportunity for the joyous solemnity and celebration that would be out of character during holy week. Therefore the Thursday after the "octave" of Pentecost is set aside for this purpose. And the feast of the sacred heart was appointed for the Friday after the octave of Corpus Christi—an octave discontinued in 1955.

The feast of Corpus Christi is of course a product of the eucharistic movement of the twelfth and thirteenth centuries—it was first celebrated in Liege in 1247. The Holy Thursday character of the feast was made clear in the bull of Urban IV, who formally promulgated the feast. The feast of Corpus Christi is basically an expression of the Easter theme, but one which seems to demand a celebration unto itself so as not in any way to detract from the Easter celebration itself.

The procession with the blessed sacrament which is associated with the feast was not a part of the original celebration. Only gradually did the procession become identified with the annual celebration, with its various "stations" and benedictions along the way. However the character of the procession was not always the same everywhere. In Germany the singing of the beginnings of the four gospels was especially popular. In fact the recitation of the prologue to the fourth gospel was so traditional that it was considered a blessing for good weather; as a matter of fact it was in this capacity that it was ultimately inserted at the end of the mass. In Rome on the other hand another aspect of the eucharist was stressed, namely that the procession of the blessed sacrament symbolized the triumphal procession of Christ the eucharistic king. This, the one generally associated with the procession today, is the theme of the living, victorious Christ—in a word, the Easter Christ whom we venerate as truly present in the eucharistic bread.

A number of objections to the eucharistic procession have been made in recent years, mainly on the grounds that Jesus told us to "take and eat" his body. Of visiting, carrying around and incensing the sacred bread, the argument goes, Jesus said nothing. On the other hand these customs sanctioned by the second millennium of Christianity have come to mean a great deal to many people. And to treat the eucharistic host with this respect is nothing other than to act on a valid implication of the real presence of Christ. The

danger comes when one stresses these customs too one-
sidedly—as has indeed happened in times past. There is
certainly a lack of balance when one prefers to look at the
host rather than eat it. And there is also the danger that we
overlook the primary reason for the real presence of Christ:
he is present to be offered and eaten.

Also we have pointed out that the Church has removed
this aspect of the Easter theme from its holy week setting
by placing this feast when she does. Part of the reasoning
behind this is that we must not confuse in our teaching and
preaching the central aspects of this mystery from those
which are less central, though perfectly valid and theologically proper.

The theology expressed in the office and mass for Corpus
Christi is magnificent in its precision and beauty. It is well
worth the time and attention one can devote to it in prayer-
ful meditation. Whether or not it was composed by Thomas
Aquinas is of no import here.

The well known prayer sung at benediction and which is
the collect for the Corpus Christi feast reminds us that the
sacrament is a "memorial of your passion." This truth is
part of the uniqueness of the eucharist, for the sacrament
which is the living body of Jesus is a constant reminder that
he did suffer for us, that he did rise again—otherwise his
living body would not be in our midst. It is this unique
instrument of God's plan for our redemption that we visit
in the blessed sacrament: the body and blood of Jesus which
suffered and rose.

The collect for the mass asks us to "sense the fruit of

your redemption." Perhaps this may best be taken to mean that through the reception and veneration of the eucharist we may, within ourselves, experience the result of the redemption which we have objectively, sacramentally experienced in baptism, and in the eucharist. In other words it is a prayer that the eucharist may do for us what it is intended to do: to make us aware of Jesus' passion by permitting us to share in it, so that we may now through the Church and later in heaven experience the fruit of the redemption. If this can be our attitude toward Corpus Christi the Church in her great wisdom will have taught us much.

## The Sacred Heart

Any form of piety which finds expression in the cult of the Church is thereby a part of the Church's worship, regardless of the legislative category into which it may fall. One such form of piety is devotion to the sacred heart of Jesus.

The most recent papal pronouncement on devotion to the sacred heart, the 1956 encyclical *Haurietus aquas* by Pius XII, gives the general guidelines for practicing this devotion. "For we believe," the pontiff says, "that if only the fundamental elements of this form of piety are seen in that clear light which comes from scripture and tradition, Christians will be better able to 'draw waters in joy from the savior's fountains;' that is to say, to realize the altogether special importance of the cult of the sacred heart of Jesus in the liturgy of the Church, in her spiritual life, and in her external apostolate."

The holy father points out that while there is no mention in scripture of any veneration to the physical heart of the lord, nonetheless it is "preached in inculcated by means of images calculated to vehemently move our hearts." Not the least of these images is that used by Paul (1 Cor 15:45) when he refers to Jesus as the "last Adam" who became a "life giving spirit" in contrast to the first Adam who became a "living soul." Paul referred to Jesus as the second Adam since, just as the first Adam was the author of the whole human race, so Christ, the second Adam, is the creator of the new redeemed race, in fact the very source of its life. Moreover, like the first Adam whose rib was fashioned into a bride while he slept, so too did the second Adam sleep on the cross, and his side was opened, and from his body poured forth the second Eve, the Church.

Thus the early Christians looked upon the Church as the mother of the living, the bride streaming from the pierced side of the savior, just as the first mother had come from the side of the first man whom God had created. "From the risen heart is born the Church espoused to Christ" sings out the vesper hymn on the feast of the sacred heart.

The Church is born from the side of Jesus! The most sublime doctrines of the faith, the Church, the sacraments, redemption and grace are here brought together in a manner which every Catholic can understand. All these wonderful realities stream from the pierced heart, the sacred heart, of the redeemer, "the font of life which spills over the

whole earth flowing from the wounded side of Christ."[1]
This is truly the sacred heart devotion in its original form.

The sacred heart devotion therefore is not something
apart from the essential Christian message. It is simply
Good Friday as seen from within, just as Corpus Christi
is Holy Thursday as seen from within. Thus it is the redemption itself—that is to say, Easter—which the feast of
the sacred heart observes through its intimate connection
with the Church. And the fruits of this devotion can
therefore be none other than those of the redemption
itself.

## Peter and Paul

The arrangement of the feasts of Peter and Paul might
require some historical explanation: for why are the two
saints celebrated on the same day, with a commemoration
of Paul on the following day?

The date for the feast, June 29, already appears in the
ancient Roman calendar of 354 in connection with the
feast of Christmas. Presumably at some earlier time on
this day the Roman Christians took the bodies of the two
saints from their original resting places and hid them in the
catacomb of Sebastian on the Appian Way. The transfer-
ence of their bodies to this catacomb was probably done to
avoid having them discovered and despoiled during a time
of persecution. It seems that by 354 the combined feast of
the two apostles was still celebrated in the catacomb, even

[1] Taken from an inscription in the baptistry of St John Lateran,
Rome.

though their bodies had in the meantime been taken back to their original resting places. One explanation for the fact that their feast days were celebrated together in the catacomb as late as 354 is that Constantine's Basilica (i.e. St Peter's Basilica) was still under construction; thus the combined celebration continued to be held at the place where the two apostles were buried together during the time of persecution.

Peter's later resting place was of course under the Basilica of Constantine, whereas Paul was buried at the Basilica of St Paul Outside the Walls. Since the people of Rome gathered at St Peter's on June 29 for the celebration, and since St Paul's was a good distance from the city—too far to have a celebration at each church—it was decided to hold the common celebration on June 29 at St Peter's, and to make a trip out to St Paul's on the following day as a special "commemoration" to the apostle. This also accords with the Roman custom of holding the celebration at the grave of the person being venerated.

## The Precious Blood

In our consideration of the sacred heart devotion we attempted to show, among other things, that the reason for the liturgical celebration of the devotion is the fact that it takes us to the core of the mystery of redemption, and that it is not an isolated article of piety. But to varying degrees this is true of every feast celebrated during the Church year, for the Church does not intend the liturgy to be a chronological following or attempted reliving of the early life of

Jesus. Rather the liturgy is the celebration of the redemption spread out for us over the span of the entire year.

Thus there is no liturgical feast of any kind which is not in some way linked with the redemption, the center of Christian life and worship. The feast celebrated on July 1 therefore, the feast of the most precious blood, must in some way be connected with this mystery.

Even a summary glance at the mass and the divine office for the feast of the precious blood reveals that the theme of the liturgical celebration is not devotion to the redeemer's blood just as such, but rather as the blood which bought us redemption. It is the blood of the new and eternal covenant, the blood of Jesus himself. "This cup," Jesus said, "is the new covenant in my blood which shall be shed for you." This is the meaning of the feast of the precious blood.

The introit for the feast begins with a verse from the apocalypse: "You have redeemed us, O lord, in your blood, from every tribe, and tongue, and people, and nation: You have made us a kingdom unto our God." The collect continues this theme: "Almighty and eternal God who made your only begotten son to be the redeemer of the world, and who deigned to be placated by his blood, grant, we ask you, that we may so venerate the price of our salvation. . . ." The epistle is from Paul's letter to the Hebrews, which deals with Jesus as the mediator of the new covenant in whose blood we have eternal redemption, and the gospel is the same as for the feast of the sacred heart—the blood and water from the side of the redeemer signify the birth of the Church. This same theme is borne out in the postcommunion.

The office of the day continues to stress the theme of redemption: "You have redeemed us in your blood, o lord." Also: "Christ loved us and bathed us in his blood," and again: "They shall conquer the dragon (i.e. the devil) because of the blood of the lamb and because of the covenant of his word."

This new covenant in the blood of Jesus, which is the meaning of the feast, must, like every true covenant, be ratified by those with whom it is made. This ratification was made by God when, in the words of the apostle, "he raised up Christ from the dead" and showed that the redeemer's sacrifice and the covenant founded therein was acceptable to him.

We in our turn ratify the new covenant every time we attend mass, and this ratification is actually expressed during the canon of the mass when the body and blood of Jesus are consecrated and offered to God the father. The laity ratify this sacred action which is the new covenant by answering "amen" to it at the end of the canon—the amen that comes just before the Our Father. This amen does not merely conclude the doxology, but also gives God's people the opportunity to ratify his covenant with them each time mass is celebrated. Justin the Martyr attached great significance to this amen back in the year 150. Its significance remains.

## The Dedication of a Church

A liturgical observance about which very little is said is the feast of the dedication of a church. This observance certainly dates from the fifth century and deserves more attention than it gets. Today of course those churches which are consecrated observe the day of their actual consecration in conjunction with that of the cathedral church of the diocese. On the day of the dedication of the cathedral church the mass and divine office throughout the diocese is that of the dedication. And all churches should join in the celebration not only of the cathedral dedication but also of their own dedication—or consecration if they are consecrated. In consecrated churches small candles are placed throughout the church, usually beneath the stations of the cross. These candles were used in the ceremony of consecration and are lighted each year in observance of the anniversary. Most of the newer churches are only dedicated. But this rite too is done by the bishop, this too sets the building aside for worship, and this too deserves to be commemorated each year.

The yearly commemoration of the cathedral (and of the parishes) is in a special way the celebration of the *Church of a given place*. So often we are accustomed to thinking of the Church as something that exists only on the "universal" level, of something that is exclusively worldwide. We tend to think of the Church as the holy father presiding in St Peter's Basilica in Rome. But while the Church is and must be universal, and while the papal liturgy certainly has a special dignity, we should nonetheless recall Paul's words to the Corinthians: "You are the body of Christ"—in other words: "You are the body of Christ at Corinth." Moreover Paul frequently refers to the Church of a particular locale,

and in the Apocalypse the letters are addressed "to the
Church at Smyrna," etc.

It is only in our day where decentralization seems to be
the order of the day that the notion of the Church as the
group of baptized Catholics who are practicing their faith
in a given locality under a duly appointed bishop comprises
the Church in that area, and that this group together with
thousands like it throughout the world comprise the Catholic Church. The Church in a given place is not some kind of
a cell of the Roman Church with the bishop as a sort of
papal vicar. On the contrary the diocese is the mystical body
of Jesus Christ gathered together under the lawful leader-
ship of the bishop who governs the Church in that territory
as its divinely appointed head. It is of course true that the
bishop received his authority from the pope as supreme
shepherd of the whole Church, and it is also true that the
bishop rules the Church there in communion with the see
of Rome. It is also true that the bishop of Rome is the chief
among the bishops of the world. But once the holy father
has made a man bishop of a certain placc, that man rules
the Church in that place by divine law as its bishop, as the
high priest of that Church.

This fact also has liturgical implications. For the worship
of the Church at, let us say, Baltimore is precisely that: the
worship of the Church, the body of Christ at Baltimore.
When a bishop of a diocese orders a holy hour held for
some particular intention, even though that holy hour is
not found in a book prescribed by the holy see, nevertheless
that same devotion is a part and parcel of the worship of the
Church of that given place. And it is so because it was

ordered by the bishop of that place. And it has no less value before God because it was ordered by the bishop for his diocese instead of having been ordered by the holy father for the entire Church.

The point of this discussion is to bring out the fact that the local Church is also worth something, and that it is only by belonging to the Church of *somewhere* that we become members of the Church of *everywhere*. The Church is only universal because she exists in separate places. And the dedication of the cathedral church and the observance of this by the parishes, as well as the observance of their own dedications, is something that is being celebrated here and now only in this particular place. It is a celebration of the Church of *someplace*. Since in the United States this is about the only diocesean clebration that we have, it should be encouraged, and properly celebrated with due attention and ceremony. And this observance should help to encourage diocesean loyalty as well as parish loyalty.

In other places, especially in Europe, each diocese has its own saints that are "diocesean saints" which are not celebrated anywhere else. This too serves to bring out the thoughts we have outlined above. In our country we do not have the patronal feasts as other places have. But we do have this yearly observance, and this we should utilize.

In addition to this local feast there are two other dedications in the Roman liturgy. First is the dedication of the Lateran Basilica on Nov 9. Since this is the "mother of all the churches" it is only proper that it be observed throughout the world. It is the pope's cathedral church. And nine days later, on Nov 18, we have the dedication of St Peter's

Basilica, the church where the pope most often presides and which, because of its beauty, size and position, has captured the world's imagination.

But it is the local feast which needs emphasizing, and it is this celebration which should awaken in us the loyalty to our individual Church, and of course to our bishop who takes the place of Jesus directly in our midst.

## Ember Days

The ember days are among the most ancient of Christian observances, although their importance seems greatly diminished today—perhaps because they are so little understood.

The word ember, like the German Quatember, is derived ultimately from the Latin designation quatuor temporum, which means "of the four times or seasons" set aside as special observances. Originally there were only three such "times or seasons" since in the spring there was the great season of lent. But eventually this fourth observance was also added.

There are a number of theories on the origin of ember days. That they are associated somehow with the harvest seasons is almost certain, especially the September ember days; yet the idea of setting apart certain seasons of the year as times of special prayer, recollection and fasting was not entirely a Christian innovation. The book of Zacharias tells of the "fasts you kept ever, when three months of the year, or four, or six months or nine were gone" (8:19). And one of the Dead Sea scrolls found in 1947 lists special exercises for the various seasons of the year.

While the idea of setting some time apart at the beginning or end of the several seasons might not have been new, still it is entirely possible that the ember days are the result of the Church's missionary policy of adaptation, for we do know that the Romans observed the harvest time with great vigor and revel. Rather than simply abolish any harvest celebration for the Christians, the Church very likely simply christianized the already existing festival by setting apart the same pagan periods as days of special prayer and spiritual exercise.

The masses said today on ember days betray their ancient character in that they contain several readings, not to mention the flectamus genua at prayer.

A good illustration of how the ember days were christianized can be seen in the history of the September ember days. These days, as the mass text clearly shows, are certainly associated with the fall harvest; they might even be called the "thanksgiving day" of the Church.

In earlier times the Saturday ember day in September was usually observed by an all night vigil which concluded over the weekend. It was probably celebrated in the early hours of Sunday and was the "ember mass." Moreover, in the early mass books, the September days closed with the eighteenth Sunday after Pentecost, which was so arranged—and still is—that it fell on or near Sept 25. All this was done in order that on Sept 25 the harvest and spiritual exercises would be over so that a pre-Christmas period could begin. This period lasted for three months, and while it was observed only in parts of northern Europe it nonetheless left its mark on the arrangement of the ember days. The pre-Christmas period began on Sept 24, at that time the feast of the conception of John the Baptist and thus so arranged as to fall just nine months before June 24, the feast of the precursor's nativity. The eighteenth Sunday after Pentecost then was a sort of "first Sunday of advent," and the epistle for the day still alludes to this fact. Truly one can say that beginning with this Sunday the Church looks toward the final coming of the redeemer and the ultimate establishment of his kingdom at the end of the world. The feasts of Christ the king and all saints are well marked milestones on this road, and it is no accident that they are placed when they are and so close together. All souls day is also included in this theme.

Ipsius sunt tempora, the ember days remind us: the seasons belong to Jesus Christ, and it is only by living them in and for him that we can hope to attain his fullness.

## The Rosary

The origins of the rosary, generally associated with the month of October, seem to lie in the custom, especially common in the eleventh and twelfth centuries, of making numerous genuflections accompanied by Our Fathers as a form of prayer and penance. Closely allied with this practice was the recitation of the psalms, in a standing position, and at each psalm genuflecting while reciting a Hail Mary. Still another factor was the substitution of an Our Father for the psalms by those who could not learn or understand them. Thus instead of reciting all one hundred and fifty psalms one could say an equal number of Our Fathers. In the twelfth century the Hail Mary became so popular that it was used as a substitute for the Our Father in the psalm devotion, and thus the recitation of the Hail Marys became known as "Mary's psalter." In the thirteenth century Dominic added the mysteries.

The feast of our lady of the rosary was instituted by Pius V in 1572, when he proclaimed the feast of our lady of victory to celebrate the victory over the Turkish fleet at the battle of Lepanto on Sunday, Oct 7, of the year before. In time this feast became known as the feast of the holy rosary and in 1716 it was extended to the whole Church by Clement XI. In the reform of the rubrics of January 1961 the name of the feast was changed to the feast of our lady of the rosary.

Of special interest here however is the selection of the mysteries and their assignment to certain days of the week. It should be noted that of the fifteen mysteries only four are feasts of Mary's role in the work of redemption. The rest are feasts of Jesus.

The first mystery is the annunciation, and the last is Mary's coronation. All the other feasts have been included not because they are feasts of Mary alone, but because they are essential aspects of the great mystery of redemption.

The five joyful mysteries are assigned to Monday, the sorrowful to Tuesday, the glorious to Wednesday. But these three days really constitute a triduum, a meditation, after the manner of holy week, on the redemption, on the Easter mystery seen in its totality. The same process is repeated on Thursday, Friday and Saturday, these three days reflecting the later medieval notion of the three sacred days of holy week. And since Sunday is always and everywhere the lord's day, or resurrection day, it is naturally assigned the glorious mysteries of the rosary.

The rosary then is a sort of popular santification of the week, just as the angelus performs the same service for the individual day. Although the bible vigil is slowly replacing the "rosary and benediction" which, together with the novena, was practically the sole form of noneucharistic parochial devotion in years past, still the rosary should and does have much meaning for us in our spiritual lives, namely as a biweekly triduum of meditation on Jesus' work of redemption.

### Forty Hours

The forty hours devotion is rooted in the very earliest days of the Christian community. For it was one of the liturgical and penitential customs of the primitive Church to observe a strict fast from the time Jesus died on the cross until the time of his resurrection.

There was of course some discussion as to how this period should be reckoned—whether from the time he ascended the cross or from the moment of his death, and at exactly what moment he rose from the dead. But the time generally observed, as Augustine points out, was forty hours. During these forty hours the faithful were expected to observe strict fast and to persevere in prayer as in vigil at the tomb of the lord.

Jungmann has observed in this connection that we today are accustomed to considered the moment of the redeemer's death on Good Friday as a signal to relax: the terrible deed is done and nothing further is necessary until we celebrate the resurrection. The early Christians however felt acutely the fact that Jesus had actually died and been buried—a great humiliation. Thus this forty hour period was strictly observed. In Jerusalem in the fourth century those of the faithful who were able to do so after the strenuous exercises of Good Friday actually did keep watch at the lord's tomb in the Church of the Resurrection.

This watch of fasting and prayer which went on for forty hours from the afternoon of Good Friday to the supposed moment of Christ's resurrection represents the origin of our forty hours devotion.

This custom can be traced continuously, though not without some variations, right up into the middle ages. In the tenth century there arose the custom in the northern countries of portraying more vividly that which had hitherto been understood and considered more symbolically.

This tendency was to make itself felt more and more as time went on, especially during holy week. While we might take a more sophisticated view of such "theatricals," they were not without their purpose as a catechetical device in an age of illiteracy and, generally, decay.

In our case the tendency expressed itself in the construction within various churches of a replica of the redeemer's tomb which the faithful could venerate and at which the forty hour devotion could be observed. This custom still lives on in many parts of Europe.

With the coming of the eucharistic movement of the twelfth and thirteenth centuries a new element was added: the blessed sacrament was placed inside the "grave" so that the body of Jesus would actually be contained. Soon however the faithful were surrounding the tomb with candles and flowers, etc. so as to obscure the true penitential character of the period. Thus devotion to the blessed sacrament had to be removed from its holy week setting and given special observance at some other time. This is the tradition that has given us the forty hours devotion in it present form.

Thus the forty hours devotion is an Easter devotion which has been removed from its original setting. But this does not mean that the spirit of Easter should be removed from the devotion, for the body of the lord honored in the sacrament is after all the instrument of the redemption, and the only explanation for the presence of the living body of Jesus Christ is the fact that he rose from the grave. The living body of Jesus is the living proof of the redemption.

## Jesus' Easter Kingship

The last Sunday of October is the feast of Christ the king. In Quas primas, the encyclical which introduced the feast in 1925, Pius XI stresses that this feast celebrates the kingship of Jesus solely as man. The holy father notes that the title king can be attributed to Jesus for two reasons: first, he was born a king; second, he merited the title by his death and resurrection. The second claim is the one of primary concern here. For the fact that Jesus merited or earned his title in his death and resurrection means that his kingship is necessarily Easter in character. In a word, Jesus is our Easter king.

The feast of Christ the king is in a sense an Easter in the fall; for this reason it is celebrated on a Sunday. And its very October setting emphasizes the fact that Easter is not confined to one Sunday a year. That the feast comes at the end of October, just before the feast of all saints, points up the notion that Jesus is king not only of the Church on earth but of the Church triumphant as well.

The mass of the feast of Christ the king excerpts from the Apocalypse: "The lamb that was slain is worthy to receive power, and divinity, and wisdom, and strength and honor. To him be glory and empire for ever and ever" (5:12). In the epistle Paul tells us how God has "delivered us from the power of darkness and has brought us into the kingdom of his beloved son, in whom we have redemption through his blood" (Col 1:13–14). And in the preface the Church sings of the immaculate victim who on the altar of the cross accomplished man's redemption.

What the Church is saying in all this is that it was in fulfilling his Easter work that Jesus revealed to the world his kingship. It was for this reason that Paul could say "I preach Christ and him crucified," and that the liturgy can sing of "God reigning from the cross." The cross itself is the symbol of Jesus' kingship. The liturgy is its most perfect proclamation.

The kingship of Jesus Christ cannot be separated from his Easter mission, for it was his Easter mission that characterized his kingship. Referring to Christ, Isaiah proclaims that "all flesh shall know that I am the lord that save thee, and thy redeemer, the mighty one of Jacob" (4:10–12). And again: "Behold his reward is with him and his work is before him" (12:10). Through the sufferings of the king, the prophet tells us, we will be healed. And Jesus himself told us on the day of his resurrection: "Did not the son of man have to suffer these things before entering into his glory?"

Another area where the intimate association between Christ and his work was long taken as a matter of course was in Christian art. For centuries the central theme of Christian art was simply the redemption itself as depicted by the good shepherd surrounded by his sheep. But even more striking was the manner of depicting Christ the king. It was always in a robe of kingly purple that the king was portrayed on his throne, the cross. It was not until the middle ages that the suffering Christ prevailed over the royal Christ in depicting the crucifixion.

But the most perfect illustration of the Easter kingship of Jesus is the liturgy of the Church. We have seen already that the Christ of the liturgy is the Easter Christ, our risen mediator. And each day the Church prays through him "who lives and reigns forever." Through the liturgy of the Church we receive the risen life of Christ which we call grace. It is his risen body which we receive in holy communion. In the liturgy Christ works and acts as he is now, today, at this very minute. And the way he is today is the way he has been since the day of his resurrection: the Easter Christ. We have seen that even on Good Friday the Church prays through her redeemer who lives and reigns forever. Our

Christ is the redeeming Christ, the only one we know. And the redeeming Christ is necessarily the Easter Christ.

## All Saints

In truth the feast of all saints is the feast of all those who, having been made holy by the sacrament of baptism and having lived their lives in such a manner as to receive the fruit of the redemption, are now in the presence of Christ the king.

Nowadays a saint is considered one whose name has been solemnly recorded in the Church's calendar by the process known as canonization. Yet Paul in his letters is constantly referring to the "saints" at such and such a place, or is sending them his greetings. Since the time of Paul predated the papal process of canonization it can only be concluded that the apostle had something else in mind when he used the term saint.

The original meaning of the word saint is simply anyone who has been made holy by baptism, and who continues to abide in the sacramental life of the Church. For the word saint means holy. In pauline usage for instance the word means "to the holy ones at Corinth." In a word the holy ones, or saints, are the members in good standing in the Church. It is in this context therefore that the feast of all saints must be understood.

The history of the feast of all saints has its source in the consecration of Rome's Pantheon by Boniface IV around the year 610. The Pantheon had been of course a pagan temple dedicated to "all the gods" and Boniface

named it the Church of Our Lady and All Martyrs. The
dedication of the Pantheon took place on the thirteenth
day of May and was a widely celebrated feast. Sometime
before the year 800 the idea of a feast of all saints took hold
in Britain and the date changed to Nov 1. This occurred
under the pontificate of Gregory IV, who reigned from 827
to 844. King Louis the Pious introduced the feast to France.

Still another date for the observance of this feast was the
octave of Pentecost, to this day the time when all the
saints are commemorated in the Greek rite. The feast
therefore is an ancient one, venerated through many centuries.

The main idea behind the feast of all saints, as we have
already suggested, is that it is another aspect of the Easter
theme, one closely related to the feast of Christ the king.
For in this feast the Church celebrates the ultimate meaning of redemption. Whereas during advent the liturgy con-
templates in general the end of the world and the second
coming of the savior, here the final establishment of the
heavenly kingdom is narrowed down to a particular aspect:
the triumph of those who have gone before us and of all
those who will come after us until Jesus comes again. And
while the Church is in truth only celebrating and venerating
those who are now in God's presence, still the feast implies
the triumph of all those who are friends of Jesus.

The feast of all souls continues the theme of all saints.
Here the Church is remembering all those who have gone
before us but who because of their human frailty are still
in the process of being cleansed from their sins before
entering the presence of Christ their king. These souls also

are living in the light of Easter even though that light may be as yet somewhat dim to them in their present state. Still it is because of the light that they are where they are and in God's good time they will live in its full brilliance.

The actual feast of all souls is monastic in origin and dates from the cluniac system of the tenth century. While the feast became quickly popular among secular as well as religious clergy, it was not until the fourteenth century that it was accepted in Rome.

The idea of saying three masses for the dead originated in Spain toward the end of the fifteenth century. But only recently was the custom made a part of the Roman rite; it was introduced by Benedict XV in 1915.

## The Liturgy of the Dead

As is always the case, the celebration of the holy sacrifice of the mass is the central manner of commemorating the dead.

One of the first things to strike us as we examine the mass for the dead is that this mass—like all masses—starts off the canon by giving thanks: "Let us give thanks to the lord our God." It might strike us as strange that at a mass for the dead the Church would be so emphatic in giving thanks.

Yet when we recall that we are in fact giving thanks for our redemption, for the fact that death for us has lost its eternal sting, we realize how appropriate it is that we here give thanks to God.

Since all of us, following Christ, hope to pass through death to life and resurrection, it is not surprising that some of the texts of the liturgy of the dead have a pronounced Easter character. In the offertory verse for instance the Church prays that the departed souls may "pass from death to life." The preface reminds us that "in the same Christ, the hope of a blessed resurrection has dawned for us." And in the gospel Jesus tells us that he is the resurrection and the life.

All these references bear out Paul's remark that, through his resurrection, Jesus is the "firstborn of the dead." Thus, although every Christian must undergo his Good Friday, his death, he also has his Easter Sunday, his eternal life in Christ, awaiting him. How appropriate then that the holy mass, which contains both these elements, should be the worship we offer for the dead.

Another interesting feature of the liturgy of the dead is its treatment of hell. Since hell only has meaning because there is something to be deprived of, the Church in her liturgy treats of hell in the context of heaven. This is clearly exemplified in the collect for the burial mass: "Forget him (the departed) not forever, but command your holy angels to receive him. . . ." And again in the same prayer: "Let him not experience the pains of hell . . . but bring him to eternal happiness."

Even the Dies Irae prays for a place among the sheep far from the accursed goats, and reminds Jesus that we and our sins are the reason why he came into the world. There is no explicit mention of purgatory: its existence is taken for granted, otherwise there would be no reason to pray for the dead.

Finally the use of black vestments and mournful music

is a reminder that all of us will some day return to the dust from whence we came. We are all children of Adam, all under the same sentence; and while we are no longer uncertain or frightened about what lies on the other side of the grave the Church would have us remember how meaningless and desperate our end would be without our risen lord.

## Thanksgiving Day

We have noted before that the central act of worship in the Catholic Church is the eucharistic sacrifice—and the word eucharist means thanksgiving. Every mass, regardless of the time of year or color of vestment, urges us to "give thanks to the lord our God." Every mass is an act of thanksgiving to God for our redemption.

Since the attitude of thanksgiving is at the very center of Catholic life and worship, there should be some manner of celebrating thanksgiving day, one of the most fitting and laudable of American customs. For this great day is not only thoroughly Christian and American but specifically Catholic as well.

The first recommendation that might be made is that there be a special mass for thanksgiving day. The text of this mass might contain references to the manner of giving thanks in both the Old and New Testaments, of the gratitude we should have for all that is ours as Americans, and finally some reference to the eucharist as the supreme act of thanksgiving. And of course the magnificent prayer by Archbishop John Carroll for civil authorities should be included somewhere in the thanksgiving service.

Moreover the mass might contain an offertory procession during which the faithful could place at the altar such things as articles of clothing as gifts for the less fortunate of the parish or community. This could easily be accomplished and is not against the rubrics. The procession could begin while the priest is preparing the bread and wine, or even at the very beginning of the offertory. And while these articles are being brought to the altar a suitable anthem could be sung.

Finally we must christianize the thanksgiving dinner. This venerable institution which was there from the beginning could be given a twofold aspect to bring it into harmony with what we have already discussed.

First, it must be given the character of a religious meal. Prayers should be said before and afterward, and it must be clear that this meal is but an extention of the great eucharistic meal of which we partook at holy mass. The dinner should be in no way somber or sad, but joyful and delicious! It should be an agape, a joyous love feast in the best sense of the word.

Second, the meal should offer the parents an opportunity to educate their children in the history and meaning of the day. In the days of the old law the youngest child present at the passover meal asked the father of the house about the meaning of the meal and the significance of the various dishes. The father responded with the story of the angel of death passing over the homes marked with the blood of the lamb; he then told of the flight of the Israelites out of Egypt and of their long journey toward the promised land.

## 5

## ADVENT, OR TOWARD THE FINAL EASTER

On the first Sunday of advent a new season of the Church
year begins, another phase of the redemption is brought
into focus. The history of advent is somewhat involved
however. For one thing there was no clearly defined idea
in earlier times as to when it should begin, or even which
feast it should precede.

The first traces of a liturgical observance of advent are
found in Spain and in frankish territory at the time of the
fourth century. But the advent of those days preceded not
Christmas but Epiphany, which is an older feast and which
had been introduced under oriental influence into the non-
Roman west. In these areas advent lasted three weeks, although the Franks later observed an advent of five weeks.
In Rome, since the time of Gregory the Great, the period
has been four weeks.

Another factor in the history of advent was the so-called
quadragesima S Martini. This was a period of preparation
for Epiphany which began on the feast day of Martin of
Tours (Nov 11) and which was modeled on lent. There
was also the question of the eighteenth Sunday after Pente-

cost—so arranged as to come after the ember days and before Sept 24, which was nine months before the nativity of John the Baptist. In the north of Europe, where all this reckoning had to be taken into consideration, advent began on Sept 25 as a preparation for Christmas. And what is now the eighteenth Sunday after Pentecost was that advent's first Sunday, as the text of the mass still indicates. Not until the pontificate of Gregory the Great was the period stabilized and the Roman system of four weeks became the prevailing manner of observing the season of advent.

## The Ember Days of Advent

The third Sunday of advent and the ember week which follows it mark the beginning of the oldest part of the Church's preparation for Christmas and the heart of the season dedicated to the second coming of the lord. However the advent ember days were celebrated in Rome long before the season of advent was observed, and most probably before there was even a feast of Christmas. They were the ember days of winter, and they were the ordination time for the Roman Church. When Dec 25 came to be celebrated in Rome as the nativity of Jesus it was only natural that as time went on these ember days were to be influenced by their proximity to this feast.

In all likelihood, here is what happened. We saw in our discussion of the fall ember days that the last ember days added to the calendar were those of spring which now fall in the first week of lent. These lenten ember days appear to have the formulas of the earliest December days, which leads us to conclude that sometime in the latter part of the fifth century the December days with their ordinations were transferred to February and these became the lenten ember days.

The readings on the ember Saturday of lent still seem appropriate for an ordination mass.

In the place of the now departed formulas, the ones containing the Christmas theme were substituted, and for nearly a century, until Gregory the Great, these days constituted the "advent" of the Roman Church.

The third Sunday of advent is characterized by the use of rose colored vestments instead of purple, and is known as Gaudete Sunday, from the first words of the introit. The use of the rose vestments is of course a much later development, an example of the frankish tendency to dramatize. Purple is the original color of the vestments used in the liturgy and it was used at all times. The theme of the third Sunday as expressed in the mass is one of joy that "the lord is near." Since the early Church lived in an acute awareness of Christ's second coming Paul was delighted at the thought that Christ's return could indeed by very near. The Church bids us rejoice also in Christ's second coming. This coming, in Paul's words, need not cause us "any anxiety."

Another interesting item of liturgical exegesis found during these days is the phrase used in the first prayer on ember Wednesday, where Christmas is referred to as the "coming feast of our redemption." This undoubtedly relates to the fact that our present manner of attaining salvation is dependent on the principle of the incarnation: the use of the created and visible to lead us to the uncreated and invisible. The humanity of Jesus, the Church, the sacraments, all are examples of this use. Thus the incarnation is the basis on which we continue to fruitfully experience Jesus' work of redemption. And the phrase is especially pertinent on ember Wednesday because the formula for the mass is in a sense a commemoration of Mary, a creature whom God used to bring his instrument of salvation into the world. The introit, the second reading, the gospel and the communion verse are all reminiscent of Mary. The fact that the station church is St Mary Major also points up this day as an appropriate commemoration of Mary in the Church's advent liturgy.

The gospel for ember Saturday and for the next day, the fourth Sunday of advent, are the same since the Saturday was originally an all night vigil which concluded with a mass early Sunday and was thus considered a mass for Sunday. The secret is also the same on both days. The formula for the fourth Sunday was added after the vigil no longer accommodated all the people; parts of this formula were simply taken from the earlier vigil mass.

Advent is a four week season of the year devoted to the preparation for the coming of Jesus Christ—not for his coming at the original nativity but for his second coming at the end of the world. Thus, just as all other seasons of the Church year are dedicated to some aspect of the redemption, so too is advent.

The Church uses the feast of the first coming to "stir up our hearts" in preparation for the second coming. And of course we pray in the liturgy for a still greater coming through grace into our bodies and souls at Christmas. It is in this context therefore that the liturgy of advent, with its constant prayer that Jesus may "come," must be understood.

The gospel for the first Sunday of advent speaks of this second coming of Jesus; so also does the gospel for the last Sunday after Pentecost, which was at one time also a part of the advent season. The pauline epistles on the third and fourth Sundays, as well as the epistles on ember Saturday and the last several Sundays after Pentecost, also allude to this theme. And the use of gospel texts relating to the great herald of the redeemer, John the Baptist, serves to remind us that God's kingdom is near. The sobriety of the advent liturgy, the use of purple (which to the medieval mind signified penance), the omission of the gloria, etc. all serve to remind us to repent, to prepare for the coming kingdom.

Advent then is dedicated to the last things, to death, judgment, heaven and hell, but above all to Jesus' glorious coming to complete his Easter work. The Church goes so far as to set aside an entire liturgical season to the end of the world and the final coming of the lord, so important a part of the faith does she consider these truths.

## Conclusion

In the course of these pages we have attempted to show that the message of the Church year is redemption. It should be clear that Easter is not so much a past event as it is a present reality, a reality which we live by the very fact that we are baptized into the death and resurrection of Jesus Christ. Since it is Easter which is directly responsible for our Christian existence it must necessarily be Easter which is at the root of our piety and Christian outlook. Since it is Easter which makes us what we are it should also be Easter which determines how we are.

Throughout the year the Church in her liturgy confronts us with Easter both in the formulation of the prayers as well as in the reality which is celebrated. This whole process should serve to form us as Easter Christians, so that throughout the year our faith and worship may be rooted in the central mystery of our faith.